HELL NO!

THIS AIN'T FOR YOU...
IT'S FOR ME!

Everyone's <u>NOT SO</u> common sense guide to staying sane in those insane times.

Written By,
Andra Leverette
(AKA Pohet)

ISBN: 978-0-578-47056-6
Editors: P31 Publishing, LLC
For more information, please visit www.andraleverette.com

Printed in the United States of America

Contents

THIS BOOK IS DEDICATED TO MY HUSBAND. I WOULD NOT HAVE WRITTEN THIS BOOK IF IT WASN'T FOR YOU. THANK YOU FOR BEING MY SOUNDING BOARD HANDSOME.

Introduction

What if I told you, I didn't write this book to help ANY-ONE who reads it, but MYSELF? What if I told you, I am writing this book so I have something to carry around to keep MYSELF in line? To keep MYSELF in check? What if I told you that I have completely and utterly made this book for MYSELF. I was, am, and will probably always be tired of these doggone self help books, that don't tell me HOW to do a damn thing. These books are so MOTIVATING! But when you motivate a fool, that's exactly what you get, A MOTIVATED FOOL! If you want something done to your liking, you have to do it yourself. The kind of self help book I was looking for, still am looking for, and will always be looking for, is something that I can carry in my purse and read, when I'm sitting in the DSHS office wait-ing for my name/number to be called. Or while I am sitting at the Social Security Office, once again, waiting for my number to be called to the next open window. Or maybe at the DMV, but NOT while I am waiting at the doctor's office with my kids for a Well-Child Checkup. For some reason, there is never time to read ANYTHING at that time. The receptionist has you fill out a 2 page form, front and back. Even though you filled the forms out ahead of time just so you wouldn't have to fill them out when you got there. But who's complaining?

Anyways, I need something that I can refer to everyday when I want to choke someone for that nasty attitude they're having with me, because someone else pissed THEM off, and now they want to take it out on ME.

I used to be apart of Amway, which isn't a bad thing. I actually liked it. See, I am a stay at home mom. My husband gave me the privilege of being at home with our children, and I am forever grateful for that, and for him. I also homeschool all 4 of our girls. Yes, you read that right. We have 4 girls, and I homeschool all 4 of them, ages 15, 13, 11, and 6. Well at the time of working for Amway, I only had 3 girls, and they were a lot younger, more like 6, 5, and 3. Because I was a stay at home mom who homeschooled, and whose husband was the breadwinner, meant we sometimes fell on hard times. I was always looking for a way to help out the household, financially, without actually leaving the house. Easier said than done.

One day a lady by the name of Susana came knocking on my door, selling Amway. I was interested because I loved the products, and I still do. Susana was in search of a downline. A downline is someone that she could sign up underneath her, and she in turn helps that person sign people under them, and so on. Yes, it's a pyramid, but I actually liked it. I signed under Susana, and then my mom signed under me, and my brother signed under my mom, and we had a few other people signed under us as well. We started attending these Amway meetings, which was fine. At the meetings they would talk about becoming your own boss, and being financially stable. They asked questions like, "wouldn't it be nice if you could stay home with your kids, instead of having to pay for a babysitter?" I started thinking to myself, that I didn't need a babysitter until I started working for Amway. Ain't that something? I kept that to myself though.

When you join the business aspect of Amway, they like for you to listen to self help cd's, and read self help/motivational books, which by the way, were VERY helpful in motivating me. I listened to the cd's everyday, and read as many books as I could. I genuinely enjoyed reading the books, and listening to the CD's, so it wasn't a problem. Well, one night I finished reading like the 4th or 5th motivational book. I laid my head down on my pillow. I was so excited for the next day, because I was about to make things happen in my life. The problem was, I didn't know HOW to make things happen. That put a frown on my face that even caught my husband's attention. My husband came to bed, saw my face, and asked, "what's wrong?" I told him that I am so excited to change things in my life, but I don't know how. I told him that I finished reading a very inspiring book, but it didn't tell me anything about HOW to implement change in my life. All it told me was, why it was so important to implement change in my life. I'm not with Amway anymore, but I seriously do think about finding someone who is, making them my upline (someone who I can sign up under), and getting this show on the road again. I've decided to pursue other things. Shout out to Amway! Love you guys and your products!

I have learned that some things are common sense. However, that common sense is different for everyone. We haven't all had the same upbringing. What may be common sense for you, may not be for me. Just the same, what may be common sense for me, may not be for you.

I began writing down my frustrations. Then my frustrations turned to observations. When something frustrating in my life would happen, I started looking at the situations as learning experiences instead. I started paying more attention to what was happening, and writing it down to reflect on it later. Once I had a conclusion, I would simply write my conclusion down, then move on. As I started doing this over the years, I began to notice that my outlook on things started to change, and so did my attitude, and my actions. People tell me, these changes come with age. I think some of these changes come with experience. Trust me, age has nothing to do with experience.

I haven't read very many self help books in the past 8 years, since leaving Amway (except for the Bible maybe).

I started writing down life experiences, and taking notes on those experiences.

I began writing these situations down as they would happen. I would reflect on what I could do differently in these situations. For example, I would ask myself if I had to say what I said with such sarcasm? Did I have to curse that lady out? Did I have to slam that door? Should I have gone back and apologized? Could I have reacted differently? Should I have kept my mouth shut?

Should I have said something or should I have let it go? Should I have confronted him or her?

I would ask myself all of these questions, and more, when something happened.

I even got to the point where I would not only write down what I could have done differently, I also wrote down the steps I needed to take to ensure that my reaction was sensible.

I decided to put my list of things to do, when reacting in certain situations, in a book. I wanted something to carry in my purse. I was tired of carrying around folded up papers that come flying out when I take my wallet out in the grocery store. It's a mess, it's embarrassing, and it's irritating as hell. I can't tell you how many papers I have lost because of this. It got to the point where I just became careless and fed up and would just throw the papers away. This is why I made this into a book.

This book is for ME to carry around in MY purse to make sure I treat people as the human beings they are. To make sure that when MY time comes to say goodbye to MY loved ones, I do not regret how I have treated them.

This was written, to help ME, help MYSELF.

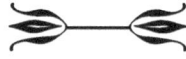

Preface: Life Begins With You

I said in my Intro that this book is for me, but I couldn't help but notice that you are reading it too.

So I might as well share with you how this works.

I am a person who believes that there is beauty in everyone. I am a person who does not get enjoyment from being greater than the people around me. I am the kind of person who wants to take everyone with me, wherever I go. I have a difficult time watching people waste away by doing things that do not make them happy. It truly saddens me when others do not perform to their full potential.

I have learned the reason why these things are not the easiest for me to fathom.

I am the one who doesn't always see the beauty in MYSELF. I am the kind of person who doesn't accept that I am indeed, great. I am the person too afraid to do the things that make me happy. I hold back, and I do not perform to my full potential. These are the exact things that I struggle with myself. Therefore it hurts my heart when I see others with the same issues.

When my oldest daughter was just 3 years old, I had the hardest time with her. I didn't know how to speak to her without yelling. I didn't know how to be gentle with her. I was heavy handed with her and had zero patience with her tendencies. In her eyes, I could never do anything right, and her daddy could never do anything wrong. One day we were at church, and the lady Minister at the church asked me how I was doing. I was honest with her, and I told her that something was wrong with me, because I didn't know if I 'like' my child. She looked at me, and asked me why? I told her all the things that I was feeling and experiencing. Everything my child did was an annoyance. Everytime my daughter asked me for something I didn't want to provide it. I didn't take pleasure in my daughters personality, and I didn't appreciate her smart ass mouth.

The lady Minister then informed me that my daughter was just like me, which is why I have such a problem with her.

I didn't take it as a compliment, because I couldn't stand my daughter at the time. Weeks later, it finally clicked. If my daughter is just like me, and I can't stand my daughter, then that must mean I can't stand myself, and maybe I am not as tolerable to other people as I think.

This epiphany made me look at my daughter differently. Heck, it made me look at myself differently. After this revelation, I cried myself to sleep quite a bit. I couldn't believe that I, at one moment in time, did not like my daughter. I hated myself for my thoughts. I couldn't believe the things I was thinking. Such a small human being that relies on me to guide and protect her.

How unfair for her. I tried my hardest to change myself. I watched how my husband would handle our daughters, so I could find out why they liked him more than they liked me. I realized that he was patient, compassionate, and displayed gentleness. He wasn't yelling at them, he wasn't treating them like he has no time for them. He encouraged their desires, and allowed them to think, and explore. The more I watched him handle our daughters, the more I saw where I was going wrong.

One night I had a dream. I dreamt that I was doing my daughter's hair, and I had black gloves on that were really rough to the touch. I saw that my daughter was crying while I was doing her hair, because of the gloves I was wearing. I was being as gentle as I could but I was still hurting her, because of these gloves. I woke up, and realized that I am simply too rough with my daughter. I needed to take off my rough ass gloves and stop hurting my child.

I prayed and prayed every night that I would have a better relationship with my daughter. I told my husband about my prayers, and he made a suggestion. He suggested that I ask our daughter why she prefers daddy over mommy.

He also warned me that I should be ready to hear the answer. The answer might be hurtful or hard to hear, but nonetheless, I needed to be ready to receive it. Not only did I need to be ready, but he also suggested I refrain from telling her that she is wrong for the reasoning she may have, and not to justify my behavior when she points it out.

My daughter was 7 years old, when I sat on the top of our staircase with her, and I asked her why she doesn't like me as much as she likes daddy?

She told me that I make her feel like she isn't my daughter. She told me, I make her feel like I want to trade her in for a different daughter.

I would be lying if I said her words didn't hurt. I looked my baby girl in her eyes, and I told her that she means the world to me, and I couldn't imagine her not being my daughter. I told her I would make sure, I didn't make her feel that way anymore. Take note, I didn't say I would TRY not to make her feel that way. I told her, I would MAKE SURE I didn't make her feel that way ANYMORE.

My daughter is now 15 years old, and I couldn't ask for a better relationship.

It took time and patience on my part. I had to be very aware of every word I used with her. I had to consciously think about my tone when I was speaking or responding to her, and I paid close attention to my facial expressions and my body language anytime we had a conversation. When it was time for discipline or correction, I made sure to reassure her that her correction wasn't because I didn't love her, or didn't want her as a daughter, it was because she did something she shouldn't have, and her behavior needs to be corrected and guided. I used a lot of explanation with her. Explaining to her why she is being corrected, and why her correction is a little different then her sisters. Yes, I made a point to make things VERY explanatory for her. That kept my tone, and voice fluctuations in check. Before I knew it, I didn't have to try as hard to be patient with her, or my other daughters. I found myself finding more creative ways to discipline, and correct my girls. My oldest daughter is now 15 years old, and she still loves her dad, but she doesn't dislike me anymore. So be it.

The reason I'm sharing this with you, is to inform you that everything you do not like in your life, or things you may not be proud of, all stem from your own actions. This is probably the most challenging concept that we have a hard time grasping in society. We are more in control of our lives than we think. We have more abilities and power than we think.

When I have a challenging day, it's normally because I didn't do something early on to make sure my day flowed properly. Maybe I woke up at 9am instead of 7am, and now I am complaining that there aren't enough hours in the day.

Everything we do has a reaction or consequence which can be positive or negative. It's up to us, as individuals, to adjust ourselves, to get the response, or reaction we are looking for.

I could have easily just kept thinking that something was wrong with my daughter, and maybe she's just not likeable. It took a lot of self control and strength, to go to my seven year old, and make things right with her. It took a lot for me to let go of my pride and realize that the child I birthed is not a nuisance to me. I had to face the fact that there was something within my own self that I hadn't addressed. I literally had to adjust my thoughts, and convince myself that I am the one with the problem, not my daughter.

This is exactly what this book is for. To help you and I adjust, so we can get the reactions we are looking for, and help identify and eliminate the problem within ourselves, so we can build better relationships.

Fix ME

My husband and I used to get into arguments that would have us using language towards each other, that would make sailors red in the face. I had a way of doing things, and my husband had a way of doing things. A lot of times, our different ways of doing things, would clash. Well one night we had an argument that was epic.

At the time, we only had 2 girls. Our oldest was 3 and our 2nd daughter was 2. We had been attending a particular church for about a year and a half. My husband and I used to have the same arguments, over and over again. It was always about the sermon that day. My husband is an avid learner. When someone gives him information, he goes and does research on it to get a better understanding, and corroborate that it was true.

This particular Sunday, I don't even remember what the sermon was about. (Isn't it funny how sometimes you can't even remember what you were arguing about, but you remember the argument?)

We left church that day, and we did our normal routine of taking the girls to McDonalds. Then we would go home and watch some TV while the girls played and had their own time; then it was bath and pajama time.

Finally, it's just the 2 of us. We're sitting and watching TV, he looks at me and says he wants to show me what he found while doing some research. I was interested to see what he found. He shows me what the Pastor said was incorrect. He showed me how the letter 'J' wasn't introduced to the English language until the 1500's. I was actually intrigued, so he showed me some more things that he found. He then asked me, how is it possible that the name Jesus was spoken before there was a letter 'J'? He then said, that there was no way that His name is Jesus. My husband was actually right. I could see the information with my own eyes. All I could think about was how this is not something that should be taken lightly. This is not something that you just walk up to people and just blurt out. I told my husband, that although I see what he is talking about, I tried explaining to him that he can't get ahead of the Pastor. As right as my husband was, I knew the Pastor was not going to take well to another man getting ahead of him, the way my husband was doing. This is what got him in trouble with the Pastor previously. Discovering information, taking it to the Pastor, and the Pastor getting so mad at him, that he would make a whole sermon on how you shouldn't get ahead of your leaders, and how you need to be able to follow before you can lead. I was just tired of the Pastor picking on my husband. To my husband, it sounded as if I wasn't supporting him. It came across as if I was just taking the Pastor's side. As much as I tried to explain to him that I'm not taking the Pastor's side, he was still convinced that I was. This argument got pretty heated. This wasn't the first time that we've had this conversation, so for my husband, this was probably the barrel that broke the camel's back. We got so loud that we woke the girls up, and they both came out of their bedroom into the living room where we were yelling. By this time, we were in each others faces. I never had a fear that my husband would lay a hand on me, so I was REALLY in his face without a care. Actually, as I look back, I applaud him for his self control in this moment, because I was really pushing his buttons.

My husband opened the front door, and went outside to get away from the argument. I know for a FACT, I was pissing him the hell off, I made sure of it. I followed him outside, and we began to yell at each other outside. He proceeds to tell me to shut up. With my pride all flared up, I yell, " Who the hell are you to tell me to shut up?!" By this time, our two daughters are outside crying, because we are yelling at each other. My husband yells, "shut the F**K up and look!" I actually stopped yelling for a minute to look around. As I did, I see our girls crying, and our neighbors are watching us through their windows. It dawned on me, that this might not look too good through our neighbors eyes. I lead the girls back inside, and let them know everything was ok. I called my mom, and told her everything that happened. I asked her to pick us up, because we needed to get out of there. I was pretty sure the cops were called. My mom literally lived 3 minutes away by car. When my mom arrived, she had my step father with her. My step father and my husband got into our car, and my mom took me and the girls in her car. As we were driving down the street for a minute we saw police cars pass us. We knew exactly where they were headed.

As we pulled into my mothers driveway, I notice that my step father and husband are not behind us. My mom notices me looking around for them, and she tells me that they probably took the scenic route to give some time to cool off. We go inside the house and get the girls put back to sleep, and my mom asks me what happened, so I tell her. My mom informs me that I'm not married to the Pastor. I'm married to my husband. I am not to defend the Pastor to my husband. I am to stand by my husband. My mom let's me know that, my husband needs to know that I'm in his corner. It's important that I take the time to reassure him that I'm on his side in those times. I thought to myself that maybe I could have said things differently to him. I told my mom that I needed to go outside for a while to think. I went outside and paced back and forth in front of my mother's house, and asked myself out loud, "what the hell happened?" With tears in my eyes, I asked "what did I do wrong?" I asked God to show me how to love this man.

After minutes had passed, I was calm enough to go back inside my mother's house. Shortly after, my step father and husband pulled into the driveway. They came inside the house, and my husband and I went outside to talk. He said that he had prayed, and asked that God fix him. I told him, I didn't realize that I was defending the Pastor, and how that was never my intention. After much talking, we both came to an agreement. From here on out, when we got to a point where we were making each other mad, we would go into our separate rooms, places, corners, or whatever, and ask God to 'fix me'.

We did just that. Arguments would happen, but no argument would get to the point of this particular night. I would say, "I need to go to another room". He would let me go, and I would be in another room by myself, for as long as I needed. Sometimes for hours, asking God to 'fix me', and to show me what he sees in my husband, so I can see it too. I would ask God to show me how to love this man. While I was doing this. My husband was doing the same where he was. I'm pretty sure he would use different wording or phrasing, but we were both off in our own corners, asking God to 'fix me'.

Till this day, we ask the One who created us to 'fix me', and help us understand each other. Needless to say, my husband and I rarely have fights now. I think our last fight was a couple of years ago.

We have gotten to a point in our relationship, when he tells me something that I don't agree with, I don't say anything. I take in what he is saying. I go into my own space, and ask for understanding on what my husband is trying to say. He does the same thing with me. We usually come back to each other within a couple of hours, or even a couple of days, and start talking about the issue. It's normally VERY civilized, calm and collected. This process has definitely brought us closer together.

The first thing I learned, that has helped me in a lot of situations with people, is to ask to be 'fixed'. Fix oneself, to be able to understand where another person is coming from. Fixed to have compassion for those who see things differently than I do. Fixed to be in civilized relationships in which another person and I are able to understand each other. Fix me so MY thoughts can change.

I encourage you to ask out loud, in your own corner, room, or place to 'FIX ME'. Whenever there comes a time that you get into a disagreement with someone, and you guys are so angry with each other that you haven't spoken in hours, days, weeks, months, or even years. Ask for your eyes to be opened to what they were trying to say to you. Ask that YOU be fixed, so YOU can change.

If you genuinely do this, whole heartedly, with intentions of wanting to change, I can guarantee you, that you will get an answer and/or an idea of what you could be doing or saying differently in that relationship.

Try it out, and see how many relationships you can mend just by these 2 words. Fix ME.

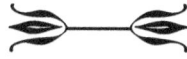

Make A List And Check It 2Wice

*L*ke I have said before, I have 4 girls- 15, 13, 11, and 6. We have been thrown into a situation where my girls have to all share one room. My 15 and 13 year old shared a room, as did my 11 and 6 year old.

We took in a few family members to help them get on their feet during some hard times, and this pushed all 4 girls into one room together, allowing for more room to be available. You might be thinking...so what? My girls are very understanding of situations, but they've had to wake up together, go to sleep together, go to school together, etc...With the girls being so different in age, you can only imagine the rise in emotions. There were arguments from, who gets to watch the television, and for how long to, when is it lights out for bed to, "stop chewing so loud" to, "stop breathing so loud".

My 15 year old gets tired REALLY early, and my 13, and 11 year old are night owls. I have my 6 year old on her own routine. So the girls are all on their own schedules, which is normal for their ages, but difficult when they all share the same room. Which is why the girls were split into two rooms in the first place.

The girls have been going back and forth with arguments about little things. As a parent, there has to come a time when you realize that your children don't stop arguing just because you tell them to. Simply telling your child to stop, doesn't always address the issue. After weeks of arguing amongst the girls, it was obvious that they are longing for some space of their own.

It was about 10 o'clock one night when I went into the girls' room to check on their status. You know, who's in pajamas, who isn't. Making sure I remind them that eventually, sleep has to happen, preferably before the sun comes up. (Hello, I have teenagers)

I look at my girls' faces, and I see that all of them are crying except for the 6 year old, she was in her own little world. I realize that they're in the middle of a heated discussion. When my 15 year old gets angry, excited, or anything emotional, tears come out of her eyes. I'm the same way. When my 13 year old sees or hears any kind of fighting, it saddens her and makes her tear up. I'm the same way. When my 11 year gets all worked up in the heat of an argument, her eyes, like her mother's, get all teary. The girls definitely take after their mother.

As I look up and see all the watery eyes, I grab a chair, and have a seat in the middle of the room. My plan is to let them carry on, as I sit and listen. I want to hear their thought processes so I can help them. I see it as the perfect time to give them problem solving tools for when they're older.

The girls continue their conversations. I just sit and listen. Sometimes, you just have to let them have at it, and get all the emotions and frustrations out. That way it's easy to hear what everyone is truly thinking, and feeling. After 30 minutes of the same argument, going nowhere, and nothing being accomplished, I grabbed a notebook, and ripped a page out for everyone, including myself, and handed everyone a sheet of paper. I stopped them mid conversation, and told them, whether they want to or not, they need to get a pen or pencil, and something to write on.

I told the girls that we are going to make a list of everything that makes us angry. Not PEOPLE who make us angry, but THINGS that people DO, that make us angry. When we are finished with our list, we will read our lists out loud.

It took the girls about 30 minutes to write their lists. I made sure to participate, so it's not about them, but about all of us.

After everyone was finished writing, we began to read our lists out loud. Each girl was allowed to read her list without any interruption, including myself. The room was silent, as we all read our lists, and some of the girls read their lists with tears in their eyes. Clearly, some of things on their lists were really close to home, and meant a lot to them.

Next, I instructed the girls, and myself, to look over the list of things you do not like, and to write down who WE have done these things to.

I asked the girls if there was anything on this list that they had done to other people? The girls' eyes widened. I told them, next to each item on their "do not like list", they are to write the names of the people that they have done these things to.

This process took another 30 minutes. To my surprise, there was a lot of giggling. When we were finished writing, we read aloud the names of all the people we have done these things to. To my surprise, there was a lot more giggling. What didn't surprise me, was the atmosphere in the room was changing. The room didn't have such a heavy feeling anymore.

When we were finished, we realized we are not completely innocent in treating others the way WE do not want to be treated.

At this time, things are a lot less tense. There are smiles on faces, and jokes are being made. It's amazing what happens when people see their own imperfections.

We didn't stop there though. Next, we turned the paper over, and made a list of things that people do that make us happy or joyful. After we finished, we read our "things that make us happy "lists out loud.

We then wrote down the people whom we have done these things for or to.

For example: I wrote, that it makes me happy when someone asks me if I need help. Next to it, I wrote down the name of someone whom I asked if they themselves needed help with anything.

If there is anything on this list that makes me happy or joyful that I haven't done for someone else, I need to find someone whom can I do it for? I need to ask myself, "How can I do this for someone else? How can I change my attitude, and/or demeanor? Am I displaying the things that I enjoy and like, towards other people?" These are questions I keep in the forefront of my mind at all times.

Once we were done with the exercise, I noticed we were all in a different mindset. We were all able to hear each other's likes and dislikes. This made it easy for us to see how much we all have in common, and also how different we are. This allowed for us to be more sensitive to each other, and help us be aware and more understanding of others likes and dislikes.

This whole process took us 2 hours but it was worth it!

The girls slept so well that night. They woke up so refreshed and rested. This exercise was so fluid. It freed up the girls' minds. It freed up my own mind. When they woke up the next morning, they looked so rested. It's amazing what happens to the quality of sleep when stress is relieved.

Here's what you need to do:

1. Make a list of things that make you angry.

2. Write down actual names of people you have done these things to, and change how you treat them accordingly.

3. Make a list of things that make you happy or joyful

4. Write down actual names of people you personally do these things for. If you cannot put a name by each item written, find someone you can do these things for.

REMINDER:

*Begin with the people in your home, then move on to your immediate family and friends.

Results

The definition of the word 'result' is a consequence, affect, or outcome of something.

A result can be a positive or a negative. The question is, what result are YOU looking for?

Right now I am literally going through a time in my life where I am on a health journey. It started out as a weight loss journey, but has turned into an overall health journey.

I woke up one day and my clothes were so tight, that even my zip up boots didn't fit anymore. This was the 'result' of me completely neglecting myself for over 4 years. So NO, my health did not get out of whack overnight. It took 4 years of me not taking care of myself, and not focusing on my health.

In 2007, after my 3rd daughter was born, I secretly suffered from postpartum depression. I never told anyone, not even my husband. I'm pretty sure he had an idea though. I had gained over 100 pounds in a years time.

It was a very difficult pregnancy. I suffered from hyperemesis gravidarum, which in short, is severe dehydration during pregnancy. This severe dehydration is involuntary. It is rare, but it presents itself as the worst case of morning sickness, EVER. Standard procedure for a woman suffering from HG is to put the mother-to-be, on hydration fluids through an I.V. for as long as she needs it. Which can be a couple of weeks, a few months, or in some cases, the whole length of the pregnancy. Every woman is different.

The next thing is to get the mother-to-be on a really good anti nausea medicine, to keep her from vomiting excessively. This is something that I have gone through with EVERY pregnancy. With my 3rd daughter, things took a turn for the worst.

I was on an I.V. for a few months so my doctor ordered a PICC line to be placed. A PICC line is an I.V. line that begins around the inner elbow, and they thread the I.V. until it gets to the heart.

My I.V. line began to grow bacteria. Now, because the I.V. line stopped right at my heart, the bacteria that was growing had gotten to my heart valve. My heart valve began growing bacteria. The bacteria broke off into particles, and those particles got into my lungs, and so my lungs had particles of bacteria in them. It got to the point where most of my body was now full of bacteria, and infections.

The doctors needed me to start eating ASAP. They pulled my I.V. line out to make sure no other bacteria got anywhere else. The problem was, I was getting all my nutrients and hydration through my I.V. line. The doctors threatened to put tubes in me to help me eat and drink, if I didn't start eating and drinking on my own. I was starting to feel as if they thought I wasn't eating or drinking by choice. After spending a month and a half in the hospital, and 10 medications later, I wasn't getting any better. The doctors let me know there was nothing else they could do for me. They set me up with as much hospital equipment as I needed, to make sure I was comfortable, and they released me from the hospital. They said whatever happens to me, at least it will happen in the comfort of my own home, and I would be surrounded by family. Needless to say, I had a healthy baby girl, and I eventually got better.

What I didn't take into account, was how traumatic the pregnancy was. During my pregnancy I was assigned a Social Worker to help us out with resources that we might need during my pregnancy. After the birth of our third daughter, my social worker noticed that I was putting on weight. I too noticed that I was putting on weight, but I didn't know how excessive it was. The social worker asked me a few times, if I'm ok with gaining so much weight in such a short amount of time? I lied and told her I was ok. I felt like my family needed me to be ok, so I said I was ok.

I started noticing that I was sad a lot. I was eating excessively, and I just couldn't seem to stop. I would just tell myself I have to eat as much as possible, to make sure that I had enough nutrients in my body to breastfeed our daughter. I went from a size 14 to a size 18 in just a few months. I just blamed it on having a baby. 2 ½ years later, my husband was taking me to Lane Bryant, and we were buying a size 22/24 pant. I thought to myself, how in the world did I get here? This was the result of not facing the truth.

The truth was, I had postpartum depression, and it needed to be addressed.

Instead of addressing the issue, which was the trauma that I had to face during my pregnancy, I paid attention to the more obvious and easier issue. My weight.

I told myself, "enough is enough". I got on an exercise routine. My husband started ordering subscriptions of ladies workout magazines, and health magazines. As a result I started losing weight. A few months went by, and I was a size 20. Another few months went by, and I was down to a size 18. The results I wanted were starting to happen as a direct result of my actions.

Needless to say, I got myself back down to a size 12/14, and I was feeling pretty good.

I got the results I was looking for according to my focus.

Focusing on my weight gave me the positive outcome or 'results' I was looking for.

On the other hand, NOT focusing on my trauma, gave me negative 'results' that I wasn't looking for.

When something is left unaddressed, it doesn't go away. It just keeps presenting itself later, in different situations, different scenarios, and you find yourself running into the exact same problem, over and over again.

Now it's November 2017, and I'm fed up with my weight once again. I got on the scale and found myself at 290 pounds wearing a size 20 pant. I prided myself on how much weight I had lost 10 years ago, and didn't even realize that I was pretty much where I used to be, but this time, I put on a lot more weight. Back in 2007, I had put on so much weight that I had gotten to a whopping 273 pounds. Now It's 2017, and I've gotten up to 290 pounds. (Boy, what I wouldn't give to be 273 pounds right about now)

Over the last 4 years, I literally watched my weight climb. Every time I got on the scale, the number would just keep getting higher and higher. I watched my weight go slowly from 180, to 200, to 237, to 250, to one day I was 275. A month later I stood on the scale and it read 290.

I wasn't sad, I was angry. I realized that I needed to address the issue of the trauma I had in 2007 with my third pregnancy. The problem was, other traumas have happened since then. My 4th pregnancy was just as traumatic. Not to mention, my 4th daughter came out not breathing, and they had to give her CPR and oxygen for 10-15 minutes before she even took her first breath of life. During the birth I had hemorrhaged significantly. It was about dinner time when they got my daughter stable, and I was finally able to rest.

My husband and I were awakened abruptly in the middle of the night by the doctors informing us, our daughter has suffered multiple seizures, and she is not breathing on her own, so they were sending her in an ambulance to Children's Hospital. They discharged me from the hospital so we could be with our daughter.

As a result of not taking care of my first traumatic experience, I didn't have a clue what to do about any others that followed.

One night, I sat down, and I made myself a prayer journal. This journal consisted of everything that I experienced in a day.

At night, when I got in bed, I would pick up my Journal and write down what made me angry that day, and what made me sad. I even wrote down things that made me happy, and things that made me proud, and things that I had accomplished that day. Whether these things were positive or negative, I would pray for guidance on how to handle whatever it is that I wrote in my Journal.

Ok, so here we were. It was 2017, and I'm cursing out my prayer journal, because I am now back up to a size 20 Pant.

I'm literally cussing in my journal because I'm so fed up with being fat. My entry for the day was "F*CK BEING FAT".

I started writing in exclamations because I was yelling in my head while writing. My prayer was, just as fast as I had put on the weight, that's how fast I wanted to lose it. Shoot, if I can put on a pound a day, then I should be able to take off a pound a day. This was literally my logic.

What I ended up doing was starting a YouTube Channel. It was about me and my weight loss journey, and homeschooling, and motherhood, and everything in between. Eventually the focus was just the weight loss journey with other little things here and there. Then it turned into a *Weekly Check-In for my Health Journey*. I had about 20 subscribers, but my goal was not subscribers.

My goal was to keep myself accountable, and share what I learned along the way.

During this time, I took on meditation. I would force myself to go on meditation walks. I walked around my neighborhood, and ended my walk by sitting on my porch for 45 minutes to an hour, just having vital time to myself. These walks forced me to think about my trauma. I found myself in secluded areas of my house, front yard, back yard, or sometimes right in the open on my front porch just crying my eyes out. It was that good crying though. You know, the kind of crying where healing happens. I spent months on these meditation walks, and talking to myself, spilling my guts to myself, and crying to myself. Eventually I cried less, and inhaled and exhaled more, and appreciated my life more, and appreciated life in general. This had become apart of my health journey.

One day while on YouTube, I came across a guy talking about intermittent fasting with a workout series he called "F*CK BE-ING FAT". I was dumbfounded.

Remember, "F*CK BEING FAT" was what I literally wrote in my prayer journal one night. I followed what he said about Intermittent fasting, and kept meditating, and I was losing weight and clearing my mind at the same time. Because of the fasting and meditating going hand in hand, I found myself addressing my trauma. I found out that I am an emotional eater. When stressful situations arise, I eat something sweet, when I feel sad about something, I crave something sweet. All this time I was emotionally eating which is why I couldn't keep the weight off.

This discovery was the direct result of me finally looking my traumatic experiences in the face, and dealing with it.

I ended up putting myself on a plan. No matter what, I had to meditate at least once a day. I had to constantly focus on my mental health, physical health, and spiritual health. For my mental health I make sure that I write in my journal, and take time out of my day to do productive things towards something that I am trying to accomplish. I also make sure that I do something that makes me stop and appreciate that I'm still alive. Sometimes it's as simple as watching a movie with my kids, or spending late nights with my husband doing absolutely nothing, and I make sure that I have night time meditation for myself to reflect on the day.

For my physical health I make sure to do some kind of exercise. I like to find challenges that only last a few days, like a 30 day plank challenge, or 20 days of walking a mile, or 15 days of squats, you know, something to keep me moving, but keeps me from getting bored too easily.

For my spiritual health I make sure that I read Scripture before I go to bed, and spend alone time in the mornings for personal silence. For me, it's those times of silence and stillness that I'm able to receive the most healing in my mind.

This is the plan that I have laid out for myself. I had to do this to ensure I get the 'results' that I am looking for. I needed a plan in place for my life.

I encourage you to pay more attention to the things in your life that may be causing some of the issues that you are having.

We tend to stray away from things that hurt too much. It's those things that hurt, that keep us bound, and keep us from the results that we are looking for in life. We tend to blame others because it's easier than looking at our own faults, hurts, or mistakes.

When I created my prayer journal, there was one intent behind it- for my life to result in constant increase. Whether it was an increase in health, wealth, knowledge, or family, I was open to whatever it brought. I just wanted increase.

My goals were to be mentally stable, healthier in my body, and to learn to face my fears, and follow my dreams.

I didn't really know where to begin when I first started my journal. So I asked myself 4 questions everyday, and answered them every night when I picked up my journal.

Here's what I asked myself every night:

1. WHAT RESULTS ARE YOU LOOKING FOR IN YOUR LIFE?

2. WHAT ARE YOU DOING DAILY TO GET YOUR DESIRED RESULTS?

3. WHAT DO YOU NEED TO CHANGE TO ENSURE YOU DO AT LEAST ONE THING DAILY, TO ACQUIRE THE RESULTS YOU'RE LOOKING FOR?

4. WHAT ARE YOUR DAILY RESPONSIBILITIES? ARE YOU DOING THEM?

Give it a try.

Activity Creates Activity

You have to put your hand to something in order to make something happen. Anyone familiar with the movie, Field of Dreams? "If you build it, they will come." Well that is actually VERY true. If people aren't coming it's because you haven't built anything yet. You're probably in the process of building. Don't get the PROCESS mixed up with the RESULT.

My brother and I are up and coming artists. Our slogan is

"The Best Damn Gospel You've Never Heard". I know you're thinking. How can you call yourselves gospel artists, yet we're swearing in our slogan? We use this slogan to express that we are real. Do our lyrics have swear words? No. Are we typical gospel artists? No. We pride ourselves in truth, honesty, and real life experience, when we create our music. We could have easily picked different wording for our slogan, "The Best Dang Gospel You've Never Heard", "The Best Doggone Gospel You've Never Heard", but we wanted to be authentic on how we felt when we made music. There was one day we were putting on a performance for close friends and family, and after we were finished performing, someone literally said, "That was the best damn gospel I've never heard". We felt the same way, so we ran with it. We call ourselves TKD613. TKD stands for True Kingdom Disciples, and 613 is for the 613 Commandments. My brother and I are probably two of the shyest people you can come across, but we want to make great music for people. This all began with a dream. No really, I literally had a dream.

I had a dream that my brother and I were waiting backstage for our turn to perform. Our entire family was backstage with us, keeping us calm, and encouraging us at the same time. The crowd was a few hundred people, and it was our first time on stage.

After I woke up from my dream, I told my husband about it, and he thought it was pretty cool. I took my brother for a drive so I could talk to him about my dream.

My brother, in my opinion, has an amazing ear when it comes to music. He was always beatboxing when he was younger, and it used to drive us crazy, but I couldn't deny the fact that he could imitate any beat that he heard.

My brother and I were driving around, and I decided it was a good time to tell him about the dream I had. I also let him know about other things I saw him doing, like writing rhymes and rapping. He thought it was pretty cool, and he was on board. We decided to make this dream a reality.

My mother was about 1-2 classes away from having her Associates degree in Arts. In my mind, she had enough knowledge to apply it. I asked her if she could coach me with my vocals. She agreed, and ended up coaching both me and my brother. Our presentation while performing was dry and stand offish. Like I said, we are both two of the shyest people, so we were not comfortable in our own skin. Our annunciation was atrocious, and I didn't have the vocals to sing a single song that I wrote. Oh yeah, did I fail to mention that I write songs?

My mother spent about 4-6 hours with me a day, teaching me how to sing without screwing up my vocals. She spent time giving my brother exercises to do, to help with his annunciation and execution on his lyrics. I was writing anywhere from 3-5 songs per day, and my brother was writing anywhere from 2-4 songs per day. We would practice these songs for hours with each other, getting used to each other's rhythm, and getting used to each other's style. Musically, we clicked early on. The only issue was, we had no music to go behind our lyrics. We practiced all of our songs acapella for a couple of years.

My father, who has been a DJ since before I was born, was excited about us pursuing music, and he sent us our very first music program. We were so excited! My brother and I could not WAIT to get this show on the road. Both of us had a hard time learning this music program, and got extremely frustrated. We also ran into a few other snags. We discovered we didn't have any equipment. We had nothing to record with, and we had no money to invest in what we were doing.

I was new to homeschooling, and most of our money went to homeschooling, so our funds were tight. We had to figure out how to redirect our finances, but still make sure our household wasn't neglected.

We ended up cutting back on certain things, and redirected where we shopped for clothing and food, to cut down on spending.

In the meantime, my brother and I were still practicing heavily. My mom was still coaching us. We decided it would be good if we performed some of these songs to give us a bit more experience. There was only one problem. I was so shy, that I couldn't sing in front of ANYONE. Not even my husband. I was so terrified to sing in front of people.

I cried out of frustration, because I just couldn't get up the nerve to sing in front of my husband.

Eventually I sang, but not in front of him. I sang in a hallway where he could hear me, but he couldn't see me.

My brother and I performed for our family every week on Sabbath for a few years. We performed everything acapella. We got real comfortable with each other and with performing. Our songs were more put together, and our presentation was getting a lot better. We recorded our first song with a toy microphone that my daughters received as a gift. It just so happened to have a plug that connected the microphone to the computer. We were so excited.

We finally learned the music program well enough to be able to make music for some of our songs we were performing for our family on Sabbath. We had been performing acapella so long, that it took time to be able to perform the songs with music. I literally had to learn how to sing in the key the music was in.

When my brother would rap, he had to rearrange his lyrics to fit the timing of the song. Eventually we got the hang of it.

A few years later, my husband suggested that we take existing songs from the radio, and songs we already knew from other artists, and rewrite them in our own words. So instead of doing cover songs, we did parodies. My husband thought this would give us a little more diversity in our writing, and technique.Each song we would rewrite, we would perform for the family on Sabbath. They got a kick out of the lyrics, and the family couldn't wait to hear what song we were going to do next. We would pull the instrumental up on YouTube, and sing or rap to the music, with our own lyrics. We did this process for a whole year. We literally, to this day, have about 40-50 songs that we have rewritten into parodies.

This process of writing parodies gave us a love and respect for all the artists that we redid. My husband was right though. When it came down to writing our own songs again, we had so much experience with so many different styles, that our music came out, THAT.MUCH.BETTER. There were a few songs that I would struggle with because it was in a key that wasn't the best for my voice. So my brother perfected his craft a bit more, and learned how to make the instrumentals himself. He learned how to recreate the instrumentals from scratch, but in a key I could sing in. Our creativity has gone up. My brother became SO confident with redoing other peoples beats, and making them his own, it was as if he had been doing this all his life. We were so comfortable working with each other at this point, that we did not even have to be in the same room to write lyrics to a song that we might have been doing together. We fed off of each other so well, that half the time we didn't even hear each others lyrics until it was time to record our verses.

We released our first CD, and sold a whopping 5 copies. (We were so excited...haha!)

Here we are, 9 years later, from the time we started until now. We are getting ready to release a few music videos for a few of the parody songs we have written.

There was also a process for the music videos. I wasn't happy with how I looked on camera. I didn't know what angles flattered me, and I didn't know what clothing flattered my body type. I made a YouTube Channel, and decided to get my confidence and experience through my YouTube Channel. I learned what angles are the best for me, and I learned what to wear, and what not to wear on camera. I also learned how to shoot videos, and edit them. Although I did this to be comfortable in front of the camera, I learned many other skills about lighting, angles, scenery, atmosphere, energy on camera, and editing with confidence.

The whole point of this, is to encourage you to do something that you enjoy. The point is to take an activity that you like, and turn it into something that you love. It's not going to be perfect when you begin. You're not going to have everything you might think you need when you first begin. You have to begin somewhere though. Nothing is going to happen for you, if you do not begin. Nothing will happen for you if you do not start. Nothing will happen for you, if you just sit around and talk about what you want to do. Nothing is going to happen for you, if you are only HOPING it someday will.

Once you begin, you will notice that people will want to help YOU. Your focus will change, and you will begin to feed whatever it is that you are doing.

Remember, I said my dad sent me and my brother our first music program, to help get us started. My niece sent me lighting for my YouTube videos. She watched my first video, and saw that my lighting was not all that grand, so she sent me my first lighting.

My husband was totally vested in our music, and he helped my brother and me get most of the equipment that we have today. He taught my brother how to shop for equipment. He inspired me to invest in a video editing program that was top of the line. We also made sure that we put money aside to save up for bigger purchases. Our focus changed. We literally, to this day, put aside a few hundred per month just for our music now. We went from recording with a toy microphone, to having 3 top of the line mics, and 4-5 more basic mics that we use, just for practice.

I want to encourage you to put your hand to something.

Here's what you need to do:

1. WRITE DOWN YOUR GOALS AND DREAMS.

2. DECIDE WHICH ONE YOU CAN REALISTICALLY START TODAY.

3. DO SOME RESEARCH ON THE GOAL/DREAM THAT YOU CHOSE TO PURSUE. (What is the first step that you need to take?)

4. BEGIN!

When my brother and I made the decision to pursue our music, I spent hours going through YouTube videos of my favorite artists performing. I used these videos to encourage myself. I used these videos to get ideas, and to learn. I watched how they performed. I am not a dancer, so I watched live performances of artists that didn't dance, and payed attention to how they kept their audience captivated, without dancing.

When it came to shooting our first music video, I watched a lot of behind the scenes videos on YouTube, and I studied them. I payed attention to what I could implement with what I already had at the time.

Believe it or not, when you focus your mind on your goals and dreams, you tend to treat people better, because you are now in a better mood. You are high off of life, because you feel like you are accomplishing something. You feel like you have a purpose. You feel like you matter, therefore, you treat others like they matter, and like they too, have a purpose.

I pray that you can get passed that fear that holds you back from pursuing your dreams. I pray that you are successfully able to put your hand to something and prosper. I pray that you are able to take a basic hobby or activity that you like or enjoy, and turn it into something that you love, and it becomes your freedom.

The Honest Truth You Didn't Know About Your Selfish Ways

his is definitely a touch and go subject for me. What I am about to explain here is something that brings me to tears, but is also one of the reasons I wrote this mini book.

My mother-in-law is someone whom I highly respect. We tend to expect more from the ones that we think highly of. There are many people I think VERY highly of, like my husband, my mother, my sisters, my brothers, and a few other family and friends. This isn't about them though. This is about what I have learned from living with my mother-in-law.

Meeting my mother-in-law was not under the best circumstances. I was pregnant with our first daughter and suffering from hyperemesis gravidarum. Hyperemesis, is the word for the excessive act of vomiting, during the pregnancy, that causes severe dehydration. The severe dehydration causes excess vomiting, and you become extremely deficient in minerals, vitamins, fluids, and nutrients in your body. Basically everything that was keeping me alive was depleted. Yes, all of this happened while being pregnant.

My mother-in-law came to visit, so she could help out. I was bed ridden at the time, and I was panicking, because I wasn't able to present myself to her as I wanted. Upon meeting her, I immediately saw that she carried herself very modestly, and she was extremely sophisticated. Needless to say, I was terribly intimidated. As the years went by, I learned that she expected the best no matter what, and nothing else was acceptable. Unfortunately, about 9 years ago, she became a widow. Her car was taken away because it was in her husband's name. Since she no longer had her husbands pay coming in, she struggled to take care of some of the bills that they had. Although she had her Social Security money every month and her own health insurance, she had nowhere to live when she couldn't take care of herself anymore.

My brother-in-law took care of her for a long time. As she got older, she became more needy and a lot more dependant on others. It became extremely strenuous on my brother-in-law, and he asked us if we could take her in. We really were not equipped to take anyone into our home at the time. We were facing our own financial struggles. I was a little hesitant to have her stay with us, because she has really high standards, and I knew we wouldn't be able to meet her expectations.

We have had the honor of having my mother-in-law stay with us for over 2 years now. There have been many tears on my part. Lot's of battles within myself on how much I can handle and how much I can't.

My mother-in-law's biggest prayer and desire is for my daughters, her granddaughters, to know, and love her as her other grandchildren do.

We live in Washington state and my mother-in-law and brother-in-law were staying in California. Nine years have passed since we last saw each other. The girls were 6, 5, and 3 years old, the last time we were all in each other's presence.

I want to make that prayer come true for her. What you guys do not know is, my mother-in-law is 80 years old and she has a few health problems. She has gout, arthritis, heart problems, and diabetes. She is on a few medications, and has many food restrictions. I am not going to get into what it has been like for family that has to take care of her, but I am going to express how important it is to have some kind of plan in place for when you are older, and can no longer do for yourself.

I am learning, as I am writing this, to not expect for my daughters to have to take care of me when I am older. I would like for my daughters to enjoy visiting me in my old age but NOT find it burdensome to bring my grandchildren over to visit me. I want my children to be able to live their lives without having the burden of taking care of me night and day.

My prayer used to be for my mother-in-law to have her own cook, who cooks things exactly the way that she likes it. That way, when she doesn't like something, it's the cooks fault, and not her family's fault. My prayer used to be for her to have an assistant of her own, so when things aren't done the way she likes, it is not taken out on family, it's taken out on the assistant. My prayer used to be for my mother-in-law to have a doctor that comes to the house everyday to check up on her, to ease her mind, and let her know that she is ok. Those were the things that I prayed for, because I had a lack of understanding, and I was, and still am, exhausted.

Now, my prayer is to be able to enjoy my mother-in-law while she is still here. My prayer is for her grandbabies to be able to enjoy her presence, and get to know her, and learn as much history from her as they can. If these burdens can be taken off of us, we would probably be able to enjoy these days that are ahead, and she too, won't have to feel like a burden. She can be the blessing that she prays to be everyday. Her prayer has always been, "Lord bless me to be a blessing".

The whole point is for our eyes to be open to the fact that, we are not preparing ourselves properly to become older in age. We are not preparing TODAY, that we may live and enjoy family, and family may live and enjoy US in our old age. We are expecting for our age to be a means, reason, and justification to act, speak, and behave any way we want, all because we are older and everyone should have to respect and tolerate that. We are expecting that because we have "paid our dues", we can treat people how we want, say what we want, and make others take whatever we dish out. This is way too much to put on our children, or ANYONE who loves us.

Through this time, I have questioned if I even like my mother-in-law anymore. Actually, I have gotten to the point where I have told her to her face, that I do not like her. The scary thing is, when I look at her, I see myself in about 45 years. I take this as foresite. As much as my children love me, I would like to keep it that way. I do not want to put my children in the position that my family and I are in right now. I started reading books on finances, and books on how to invest my money properly. So far, my favorite book is The Wealthy Barber by David Chilton. There is a chapter in the book that talks about wills, and burial money, and things like that. This was such a difficult chapter for me, that half way through, I closed the book, and didn't pick it back up for 2 months. I just couldn't face the fact that when I get older, I am literally in position, right now, to need my children to completely take care of me, when I can no longer take care of myself. I cried myself to sleep many nights with the thought that they are going to hate me when I am older. My children's last memories of me are going to be how much of a burden it was to take care of me before I died. That thought made my whole being plummet to the floor, in disappointment and disgust with myself. I realized that I am failing my children. If I can't prepare properly, how are they going to learn how to prepare, and teach their children to prepare, and so on. After a couple of months of depression, a fire was lit in me. I needed to start shaping my life. I needed to make sure this does NOT happen to my family. I was also determined to give this same security to my mother-in-law.

It dawned on me, that MY mother-in-law may not have realized, that this was what she prepared for her life. It occured to me that she doesn't WANT to be in this position. She is in this position because she did what we are all taught to do. Get insurance, and plan to retire. No one ever tells us to plan for when we are older, and cannot do anything for ourselves anymore. Unfortunately, there is nothing that she can do about it right now. What's done, is done. So I am literally taking it upon myself to make sure that her family's last memories of her are NOT of a burdensome nature, but of joy, love, and nourishment to everyone involved.

This, ladies and gentlemen, was the fire put inside me, to write this book.

My Prayer

May we all stop what we are doing, and not only think about tomorrow, but think about our old age. May we plan to grow old, and not live everyday like it is our last one. May we live everyday anticipating growing old, and being full of wisdom, and seeing our children's children, and our childrens' children's children. May we see our selfish ways and turn from them.

So be it.

Outro

I have shared every key point, that I found important so far. I have shared with you some of my deepest, darkest moments. Moments that I am not very proud of, and thought processes that I'm not very proud of, but still felt the need to address. I am not the only one, on this beautiful land, who has these issues, and struggles. Some of you have far worse things that you are dealing with. I just wanted to be able to provide something that can help you keep your sanity through these challenging times that we are all facing.

I also wanted to make sure that my children had something to look back on when I am not here anymore. They can see what I was thinking, and why I did some of the things that I did. So when they have to face challenging times of their own, they have something from their mother, to focus on. I wanted my children to not just have memories of their mother, but to also have something physical to look at. Something that they don't have to try to remember, but something that they can pull off their shelf, open it up, and read. If they lose it, they know where to get another copy. I didn't want these things to die with me.

This is only the first book. As long as I'm still alive, I will make a second, third, fourth, fifth, and so on…

May this increase your thoughts.

May this increase your health.

May this increase your life.

May we all be increased with health,wealth, and prosperity.

SHALOM

About The Author

Andra Leverette was born and raised in California. Her mother moved their family to Washington state when she was 12 years old. She currently resides in Washington.

Andra is married with four daughters. Andra is a stay at home mom, who not only homeschools all four of her children, but pursues a music career, and a career as an author. Andra also goes by the name Pohet (pronounced poet), a name she took on, after her husband created a character in a book series he was writing. The character was based off of Andra. He named the character Pohet. She has taken the name Pohet, and is currently using it as a stage name for herself, and her younger brother's pursuit of music. Andra is also dabbling in other endeavours that she has not yet made known.

Andra's motto:

What if life ISN'T short?

What if tomorrow IS promised?

What if we have it all wrong?

Plan to grow old.

.

www.ingramcontent.com/pod-product-compliance
Lightning Source LLC
Chambersburg PA
CBHW031220090426
42740CB00009B/1245